Praise for This Book

This book is full of valuable advice for kids—about choices, consequences, choosing friends wisely, speaking up when you witness something bad, not chasing the approval of others, having self-worth, self-esteem, and self-love, and so much more that kids need to know to armor themselves against the vicissitudes of life.

—Sherry Moss, parent and teacher

Carole Longmeyer brings yet another gem for young readers: How to Be a Good Kid in a Rotten Apple World. She reveals her personal struggles as a youngster, guides the reader through a discussion of good and bad, and includes a list of life coping strategies. Parents, teachers and guidance counselors will also find the book useful with students, as a springboard for discussion through such topics as avoiding conflict, anger management, avoiding drama, and nourishing fruits of the spirit: love, joy, peace, patience, kindness, goodness, faithfulness and self-control. Throughout, one will hear the author's voice of love of life for people.

—Bonnie Brown, former reading teacher

Full of good advice...very timely...easy to read...speaks to kids like their grandma does...traditional American values expressed so today's kids can easily understand them.

—Forrest Schultz, book reviewer

I LOVE this book! It's insightful, delightful to read, relevant to the world we live in and kids are going to benefit greatly from it! Inspiration at its best! The checklists at the end will give kids a platform to make better choices and grow as human beings—especially those kids who were dealt a sorry hand in life.

—Joanie Vilcheck, parent, grandparent, nurse

This book is so necessary! Kids today live in a confusing world, and it's hard for them to know what is REALLY right, and who may be SO WRONG in their actions. All adults are not excellent role models—some are just mean, uncaring, and make bad choices that children are then left to see. So, how are kids supposed to know how to act themselves? This neat book takes a great stab at this issue: what are the values kids today should have, and how should they deal with those adults around them who are making poor choices? There are lots of good suggestions here that should make kids stop and think about the person they wish to become as they "grow up." As the author says, it's sad that we even have to discuss these real, but terrible, tragedies that have occurred in our country in the recent past, but the reality is that we do have a Rotten Apple world more than we would like to admit. Our kids are the strength of our world and they need all the help they can find to make good decisions for life. Read and learn.

—Fran Stanley, former teacher, pediatric nurse and child advocate

This book is really needed at this time. While many children get this kind of insight and advice from their parents and/ or extended families, the sad truth is that too many others do not. This is a wonderful way to reach out to those children—and to reinforce clear-thinking and good values in the kids who have already been exposed to it. Ms. Marsh offers an invaluable gift to kids. This book speaks the plain truth about life in language that's clear and honest, while still being respectful and caring. It's more than a simple wish for kids to have a happy and fulfilling life, it offers them the tools to achieve it.

—Kathy Dean, Contributing Editor,
Springs Publishing

How many times have you heard "What are you going to be when you grow up?" or "What do you want to be when you grow up?" In this book, Carole Marsh asks a question deeper and more important than WHAT you plan to be. Her question is "HOW do you plan to be when you grow up?" Just as it is your choice what career path in life you decide, it is your choice on how you will live out your life. This thought-provoking book stimulates the reader to begin mapping the inner true north of one's character. Decide now and know how you want to be, for if you continue to aim at nothing, you will hit it every time.

—Susan Merrill, Director of Fund Development,
Girl Scouts of Greater Mississippi

Love this straight-talking little book, filled with humor, personal anecdotes and tools for kids to arm themselves with when they encounter "rotten" situations. So many specific situations and ways to handle each, make this a valuable resource for kids. And it's easy to imagine my 10-year-old grandson and 11-year-old granddaughter finding this a fun read! WIN-WIN! The perfect "assigned reading" gift from gramma!

—Glenda Harris, author and book reviewer

How to be a Good Kid…In a Rotten Apple World is a bright light in a modern world that no longer values the teaching and beliefs of the past. But, author Carole Marsh does. She not only describes the pitfalls of life and how to avoid them, but tells her own story of shortcomings and problems that most people tend to avoid in today's society. Carole writes about how character, self-discipline, and individual responsibility are the keys to being "good" when others aren't. As a father of two young ladies, this book would have been a tremendous help when they were younger. In fact, it would have been a big help when I was growing up. Thank you.

—Tommy Webb, production manager,
Red Cross Blood Drive Coordinator, and
United Methodist Church youth leader

HOW TO BE A GOOD KID — IN A — ROTTEN APPLE WORLD

CAROLE MARSH LONGMEYER

GALLOPADE

GAWK™
God's Awesome Wonders for Kids

How to Be a Good Kid in a Rotten Apple World

Design & illustrations by Susan Van Denhende

Published by Gallopade International,
Peachtree City, Georgia USA

BISAC: JUVENILE NONFICTION / Social Topics /
Self-Esteem & Self Reliance

For premium copies, trade information, review quotes, or
other, contact michael@gallopade.com.

Other Books by Carole Marsh Longmeyer

FIRST AID FOR IGNORANCE

How to Survive Getting an Education and Stay Off Financial Life Support!

WHO YA GONNA CALL?

The Kid's Directory of Self-Help

TOUGH STUFF FOR KIDS 7-17

SMART SEX STUFF FOR KIDS 7-17

A Book of Practical Information and Ideas for Kids, Parents and Teachers

THE PARENT AND TEACHER'S GUIDE TO HELPING STUDENTS NAVIGATE THE BUMPY ROAD FROM SCHOOL TO MORE SCHOOL, FIRST JOB, AND CAREER

Table of Contents

BELIEVE THERE IS GOOD IN THE WORLD

"God has nothing to make men and women out of but boys and girls." —Lucy Craft Laney

A Word From the Author

Hello, Kid, Pre-Teen, Teen,

Hey, so you think I wanted to write this book? No! Of course not. But really, I'm disgusted. There's an awful lot of bad in the world these days. (Actually, there always has been.) Unfortunately, the media dishes out more bad news than good, so we don't see that the majority of moms, dads, girls and boys, teens and young adults are good. Some are very good. Some are superheroes!

It's hard to notice this sometimes when what we see and hear is about rotten apple stuff like kids killing themselves after being bullied. Or about cops (whom I prefer to call police officers) shooting people without a good reason. And road rage—how weird is that? And then there's this sick dude who wants to nuclear bomb the world. Why? Nothing's funny about bombs. Or terrorism. Or war. Or road rage. Or bullying. Or doing drugs. Or shooting kids at school.

And don't get me started on adults. If kids can be good (or bad), adults can be good or *BAD*. How are you supposed to know what to think when adults are racists? Or do drugs? Or are criminals? Or are just plain mean, hateful, molesters, or worse?

Why should YOU even strive to be good? And *how*, when good is not always cool, and not easy when even kids can be cruel, hateful, and mean?

All good questions. But there are answers and reasons and strategies. You can be good, and being good can be good for you, your future, and the world. Read a bit of this book and see if you agree. I'll try not to be too long-winded, preachy, or boring.

Carole Marsh Longmeyer,

Former Kid, Pre-teen, Teen, etc.

A Personal Reflection

You see, I like to write "up" to kids, to respect you. So I found it interesting when some adults disagreed with the premise of this book, that it's often a rotten apple world. Actually, I wanted to agree with them; I really, really did. I mean I was a good kid when I was a kid. (Well, more or less; you know how it goes!) And I think my grandkids (who range in age from six to twenty-three) are perfect, naturally. I think if you are even bothering to read this book, you're probably a good kid, too. But I know that even good kids have a lot of bad stuff happen to them, or they see bad stuff, or worry about bad stuff happening. I know.

When I was a young kid, my mother was the "baby" of our family. My sister and I sort of lived on the sidelines of her limelight. She had mental problems, and they did not treat those any better back then than they seem to do now. So we suffered a lot as a dysfunctional family. There was frustration, anger, fear, lonesomeness, misery, and tears.

I would like to say that school was my sanctuary, my respite, but it was not. I had terrible eyesight and did not get eyeglasses until the ninth grade. So I spent every school day struggling to learn to read and write, not because I was not smart, but because I could not see. I could not even read a STOP sign at twenty paces, so the blackboard was my nemesis. I sharpened my pencils constantly to memorize as much of the board as possible. But in sixth grade, when I was asked to read aloud from the board (from the back of the room), I had no choice but to make up some gibberish. The teacher was angry and assumed I was rebelling or a troublemaker. The kids all laughed at me. It was a new school for me (my, let's see, hmm…my sixth in as many years). Why didn't I just say that I could not SEE? I imagine many of you have tried that. "Hey, Ms. Jones, I can't read the board; I need to sit in the front row." Yeah, right. I no longer bothered.

I was quiet and shy, did not have many friends. Well, I had one. I did not feel like anything was for me. My mother did not let my sister and I have friends come over much; no overnights. We didn't even have friend birthday parties. We just sort of existed. Church might have offered some peace or instruction or something else helpful, but we infrequently attended a Southern Baptist church that was all "hellfire and brimstone." It was a scary place, the only consolation being cookies with holes in them for a snack.

My teachers were not helpful, I hate to say. (I do love and appreciate teachers, but I just did not have many good ones.) It wasn't so much what they did; it was what they left out. Although I was a good writer at a young age, I did not get any praise. The teachers catered to their pets or the kids with personality, not shy kids like me. And not one ever helped me see my potential, a career path, or even tell me I should go to college. Neither did my parents. I was lost.

So, no, I did not get beat up (too much), or molested (too much), or shoved around (too much) But I did get short-changed, ignored, and left to my own devices, which mostly was loving to learn, but being a sad and lonesome outsider.

In tenth grade, things got worse. We were at school when the principal came on the PA system and announced that President John Kennedy had just been assassinated. It was devastating. What kind of a world was that? It was bad enough that we had "stop, drop, and roll under your desk" drills back in elementary school—in case of an atomic bomb. (Uh, like that was going to help us much!) And I lived in a downtown neighborhood in Atlanta where many of our neighbors were Jews who had escaped the Holocaust. Many of them had numbers tattooed inside their forearms. My Jewish friends did not have grandparents, or aunts and uncles; they had all died in concentration camps.

So, yeah, it felt pretty much like a rotten apple world.

I can't speak for other kids—not you, not my own kids, not my grandkids. I just know that there are ages when you feel there are a lot of rotten apples in the world barrel. You scratch your head because you know there are good people. But when you learn that an Olympic doctor has molested girls over years…or see kids who need a lot of mental help get none and so they shoot up a school…or watch some world leaders act like little kids having temper tantrums, well, you might wonder—why bother being good? How do you be good when the odds feel stacked against you?

That's what I want us to look at. I can say that when you hang in there, things can change for the better. And that is a very good thing.

PART ONE:
No Goody Two Shoes

Shhh…

I think I know a secret about you. You really want to be good. Even if you think you are bad, you secretly want to be good. You might even desperately want to be good.

Why would you want to be a good person? Because it's good for YOU. Most people in the world are good. They are the people who make the world go around. You know a lot of them. They may not be your mother or father, teacher, or the kid who sits behind you in class. This does make things hard.

Or you may be lucky enough to have a good parent, good friends, a good teacher, but maybe those bullies at school really get to you.

When you're real little, it may be easy to be good. But the older you get, the more you run into stuff that can make you angry, jealous, bitter, scared, insecure, and a whole lot of other aggravating, frustrating, and confusing stuff.

The next pages have some tips, thoughts, stories, and strategies to help you be good in most circumstances.

After all, it's often not survival of the fittest, but the goodest kid that comes out on top in this world. Really.

And you don't have to be a goody two shoes to be good.

Good on Him!

A correction's officer on vacation spotted a seven-year-old trapped in a pool, drowning. He set his own child down and jumped in the pool with all his clothes on. Not only did he try to get the boy (who was stuck in a drain) out of the pool, he stuck his head under the water and gave him CPR until they could get him free of the drain and out of the pool. Smart thinking!

Good for You!

You know what good is whether you want to admit it or not.

The Golden Rule from the Bible gave us a big hint: *Do unto others as you would have them do unto you.*

There's also that Ten Commandments thing. You know, like honor your mother and father, don't lie, don't steal, don't kill, and such. (Most religions have a similar Do Good list.)

But more than that, you just KNOW what being good is. It's as simple as being nice. Polite. Sharing. Not saying nasty things. Don't tease. Don't bully. Simple stuff like that.

But when you're on the receiving end of bad stuff like a not so good parent, a mean teacher, hateful kids, or worse, you may want to give up being good and just be bad yourself. Why not?

Making the wrong choice at this point can be a big mistake.

It could change your whole life. It could even end your life—before you get to the good parts.

Don't do that to yourself. Even if you are bad now, or a bit bad, or don't want to be the kid who is different, left out, a geek (or whatever the word of the day is), don't even think about it.

NOW is the time to find reasons to choose to be good—they are often right under your nose and you don't even see them. If you're good, stay good, in spite of everything. And if you've been bad, well, no one says you have to keep it up. You can change; you're allowed.

A Spectrum from Bad to Good to Great… IT COULD HAPPEN!

rotten to the core

ordinary bad apple

chooses to be bad

plain old apple

chooses to be good in spite of things

gangs up with good instead of gangs

decides to make good choices, for better or worse

BAD
GOOD

Good Might Be Boring, But Good Is Safe

When I was a kid, I had to be good. Kids were supposed to be seen and not heard. We had to say "Yes, Ma'm" and "No, Sir." We had to ask to be excused from the table. And a lot of other stuff. *Boring.*

I could see that being bad often meant a kid ended up in the principal's office, or even getting expelled from school. Being bad was not cool. But bad kids seemed sort of cool, and exciting. I felt sure they were having a lot more fun than I was.

But I was a chicken-livered kid, so it was easier to be good. I crossed paths with bad: flashers, bullies, cheaters, thieves, the kid with the knife, the girl who was pure mean, the boy who was dangerous, and adults I did not feel so good about. Nonetheless…

Those were more innocent times.

Today, good is a safer bet than bad. Even for adults. Many adults make awful choices. You can learn to be good by *not* doing what some adults do!

There's a lot of peer pressure to be bad, sometimes. And why not? The bad kids want to bring you down to where they are. They may have a lot of problems and they may not have much of a future. And so, they don't want you to have one either. Are you going to let them make that choice for you?

No.

Dumb and Dumber

There are a lot of ways to be bad, even evil. But being a dumb bad person just sort of takes the cake, don't you think.? Don't be the thief who looks right into the security camera when robbing a store. Don't be the hit-and-run-driver who hops out of his car to get away from the cops...and runs in front of his own car and gets run over! Don't grow up and be the kind of world leader who says, "Well, I'll just push that nuclear button and blow up the world. They'll see!" Right—we'll see that leader finally realize he lives in the world too, so "poof!" dumb guy! There's heartbreaking dumb, too, like the guy who had road rage and shot a girl he thought was trying to get in his way; he killed her. She was just lost. And then, so was he, as in life in prison with no parole ever.

GOOD+DUMB IS BAD.

BAD+DUMB IS A DISASTER!

Being Bad Today

Being bad today is just too scary. It's not like the old days when a bad kid might say a bad word. Or tease someone and hurt their feelings. (Oh, wow.) Or shoplift an apple off a cart.

Today, being bad can involve words that hurt someone so badly that they kill themselves. Being bad can involve drinking, doing drugs, bullying, joining a gang, or many other things. Some of these things you can go to jail for. Jail is not cool, fun, or exciting. (Ask someone who's been there.)

Being bad today can ruin your life tomorrow—as in *forever*.

I don't think you are Good one day and Bad the next. It's a process, a habit. If you have the Good Habit, keep it up. If you have the Bad Habit, break it before it breaks you.

The Gray Area of Bad

Where's the precise dividing line between good and bad? LOL, there's not one. A good plan is if you find youself moving into the gray zone, move back out. You can piddle around in the gray zone and maybe get lucky. (Of course, a lot of kids doing drugs for the first time found out this was not a precise science since they ended up at the morgue.) That gray area is not as wide as you might wish. People who are "accomplices" and never held the gun or pulled the trigger find out that gray might as well be pitch black. So stay out of the gray zone or get out of it quick as you can. Once you go all the way to the "dark side," you might not be able to come back to good, not even if you want to.

Don't Play With Fire

A lot of kids go astray like this: "Oh, look at that smoke. It looks interesting, it smells good; I think I'll check it out. Oh, wow, now I see a flame; it's pretty even though it looks hot. I think I'll just get closer and see what's going on. I'll be careful. Gee, here's a blazing fire! It's bright, scary, but enticing, even beautiful. I'll just get a little bit closer. I'll be ok; I can always run away if it gets too hot or too dangerous." Soon, that kid finds out that you really can't play with fire. Once you get too close, it can engulf you. Steer clear of "fire" whether that's drugs, bad relationships, petty crimes, or anything else that can so easily ensnare you. "Hey, I think I'll just stay across the street or go on home." That's a good idea!

Why *Are* We Bad?

Sometimes, we're just acting the way people around us act. That might be parents or other relatives, or our so-called friends.

Other times, we might be afraid, or insecure, or feel like the only way to get along is to act tough, bully, or at least pretend we are bad. But before long, such bad habits become long-term bad habits.

If we do bad things, we get a bad feeling about ourselves. We then believe we are bad and so we do more bad things. You might not have started out with the idea: "Hey, I think I'll be a bad kid." But there you are.

You CAN get un-bad.

un-bad

Getting un-bad can be hard. I truly admire prisoners who finally end up getting an education behind bars. who serve their time (often a long, long time) being as model a jail citizen as they can be. often, they really do learn skills, morals, values, and end up becoming the person they either always wanted to be, or never even suspected that they could be. But don't make it that hard on yourself. Count your blessings (such as they may be) each day. And if one of them is that you are not in jail or prison, well, that's a good start!

No Rules

Let's get something straight:

- You can be pretty and be bad.

- You can be poor and be good.

- You can smile sweetly and be a real con artist.

- You can look tough and actually be a wonderful person.

You can't really look at a person and tell if they are good or bad by their looks, but you sure can tell by their actions!

Good on Them!

There was a 103-year-old woman in a nursing home. Someone asked her, "What do you need?" She said, "A kitten." In spite of all the RULES, she was given a kitten, which she loves, and that is always at her side, making her happy and less lonesome

---

Who Are the Good People?

Here are some people. (These are adults.) Draw a good or bad conclusion about each one:

Javier is considered to be ugly. He has scars on his face, and a scowl most of the time. *Is he good or bad?*

Eleanor walks with a limp. She does not smile much. She has shifty eyes. *Is she good or bad?*

La'Creva is a teacher. She seems grouchy a lot of the time. She is tough on her students. *Is she good or bad?*

Poker has tattoos all over his arms. He is a bit scary-looking because he is so tall and muscular and has a beard and piercings. He drives a motorcycle. *Is he good or bad?*

TURN THE PAGE TO FIND OUT.

ELEANOR

Javier is a firefighter. He was burned once in a fire. But he is the first to roll out when the siren blares and he has saved whole families, and many kids. He also makes a mean pot of chili in the firehouse. *I'd say he's a good guy, wouldn't you?*

Eleanor has had a hard life. Her husband abused her. She is a cook in a school cafeteria. She makes the best brownies the students have ever tasted. She is always looking around to make sure that every kid gets one of her brownies. *She is as good as gold.*

La'Creva is indeed a tough teacher. She drives her students crazy. But they learn and they pass their tests and they go on to the next grade and they really do learn to read well, write well, and do math and science pretty well, too. Later, kids admit that she was their best teacher ever. *She's good.*

Poker is quite the character. He works in a hospital emergency room. If you come in on a stretcher from a car wreck, he is the one who tenderly lifts you onto a bed, and if you need surgery, he sees that you get to the operating room pronto. He also checks on you later, and slips you a candy bar as soon as he knows that's ok. He's also funny and sweet and takes care of his elderly mother and knits blankets for the babies in the nursery. *Good, good, good.*

MOST PEOPLE ARE GOOD. YOU CAN'T JUDGE A BOOK BY ITS COVER. WHEN YOU ARE RUDE OR MEAN TO PEOPLE BECAUSE OF HOW THEY LOOK OR DRESS, YOU MIGHT HAVE JUST BEEN MEAN TO A PERSON WHO SAVED A LIFE THAT DAY, OR PREPARED A MEAL FOR THE HUNGRY, OR HELPED A KID IN NEED. (Oh, dear, who would be the bad dude then?!)

Who Are the Bad People?

Sometimes, it's hard to tell.

(Hey, you know how this works now, so just enjoy it!)

Malcolm is a handsome man. He wears gorgeous suits. He drives a really cool car. He has a penthouse office.
Is he good or bad?

Tybrissa is an actress. She has made a lot of popular movies. She is beautiful. You see her in magazines all the time. She can sing and dance, too. And she has gorgeous children.
Is she good or bad?

Zo is so smart. His IQ is off the chart. He owns several businesses. He goes to church each Sunday. He donates to charities. *Is he good or bad?*

Coco is a petite person, always with a smile. She lives on a farm in the countryside and has many visitors who always leave with a puppy. *Is she good or bad?*

TURN THE PAGE TO FIND OUT.

MALCOLM

Malcolm is a thief. He steals pension money from unsuspecting retirees who trust him. He soon ends up in jail for bilking them out of all their life savings. *Bad, bad, bad.*

Tybrissa is not good to her beautiful children. She sends them far away to different boarding schools that they hate. She does not let them come home for holidays. She forgets to send them gifts or money for things they need. The kids are lonesome and sad and miss each other. They feel like orphans. *Not so good, huh?*

Zo makes so much money that he can afford to donate a little bit of it to charities to hide that he is using most of his money to buy arms to give to terrorist groups. These weapons have been used to kill many innocent people. *Badder than bad.*

Coco raises puppies on her "farm," but they are part of a horrible puppy mill, where dogs are abused. *BAD!*

THE TRUTH IS BAD PEOPLE AND GOOD PEOPLE LOOK A LOT ALIKE. YOU CAN'T JUDGE BY APPEARANCES ALONE.

GOOD OR BAD IS NOT HOW YOU LOOK, IT'S WHAT YOU SAY AND WHAT YOU DO.

Look in the mirror. I know you're a kid, but do you see someone good and staying good, hovering between good and bad, or mostly bad and heading toward being an adult like one of those bad ones noted above?

Another Personal Reflection

I have done thirty years of school visits. During that time I have met a lot of good people. Here are just a few:

- A teacher who worked with migrant children by providing educational materials right in the fields, when their parents could not send them to school.

- Some teens who asked me how they could grow up and not make mistakes like those that caused the *Challenger* spacecraft disaster.

- A grandmother who worked as a baggage handler at the airport so that she could raise her three grandkids after both of their parents overdosed on drugs.

- Three brothers who went home from school every day to milk the family's cows before they went back to school to practice for the football team.

- A seven-year-old African American girl who asked me to tell her she could grow up and be a police officer. "A policeman shot my brother," she told me. "I want to be a police who does not shoot someone's brother."

- A young man who traveled halfway around the world to tell me that I changed his life. He said my books made him love to read and want to become a teacher.

And so many more. There are so many more good people in this world than bad. You may not realize that you meet them every day. Look around a little bit harder!

Author Carole Marsh Longmeyer Says

"There is only one thing to do to help the world become a safer, kinder, smarter place—for each of us to build ourselves into better human beings through knowledge, friendship, and a focus on fairness to everyone."

Strategies to Help You Stay in Good Standing

AVOID CONFLICT

There is nothing good about conflict. Everyone has an opinion. Opinions can be different; get used to that.

Everyone argues. A mild disagreement or a minor argument is normal. Intentionally ratcheting it up into a full-blown life-or- death fistfight, knife fight, or gunfight is *not* normal!

Anything that involves hitting, spitting, screaming, pushing, shoving, threats, or worse, is the kind of conflict that can get you in bad trouble. You can start out right, but end up being wrong, the bad one, and in trouble.

Don't build a habit of conflict.

Avoid Conflict:

Walk away. You don't *have* to answer, to argue.

Be the calm one. It's no fun to argue with a *calm* person.

Stay away from people that you already know make you angry or pick arguments with you.

Practice conflict avoidance. Sometimes, a simple, "Yes, ma'am," is a good way to avoid further conflict.

You are either part of the problem—if you can't resist turning a minor disagreement into a major conflict. Or you are part of the solution—if you can keep your head, stay calm, laugh something off, or walk away.

Good is to avoid conflict.

Bad is to make conflict a habit. Someone's gonna get hurt sooner or later, *probably you.*

Dumb and Dumber II

The news headlines, Facebook, You Tube, etc. just say it all. People can be really dumb. People die over dumb things. "He dis'd me!" "She stole my boyfriend!" "He pulled right in front of me!" "So I shot him!" "So I stabbed her!" "So I..." It's just dumb! Be good or be bad, but please don't be dumb!

Skip the Drama

A lot of people think drama is fun, good, exciting.

You might think that because you see a lot of drama on television, the Internet, or in movies, that drama is normal. It is not. Drama is usually made up. Real life has enough real drama (cancer, war, etc.) without fabricating fake drama.

"Oh, my gosh, it was a giant snake and then it bit me and I had to go to the emergency room and they almost had to sew my finger back on and it was my friend's fault because it was her pet snake and she left its cage door open on purpose so it could climb in my bed and bite me! And I hate her and I'm going to sue her!"

All that may be true. But the truth is that it was a fishing worm, and it was in some dirt, not a cage, and it never got in a bed and it never bit, but it scared you and so you ran and tripped and fell and had to go to the Urgent Care to get two stitches.

We all exaggerate, but making a mountain out of a molehill is a bad habit. It is sort of like a lie. Lying is bad. No one believes you after awhile, like that boy who cried "Wolf!" once too often.

Drama is bad. It's exhausting. It's not as good as a good life full of not-so-much drama. If you do a lot of "he said" and "she said," then you will end up with drama, not truth.

It's bad to create drama that turns into a lie that gets someone in trouble. That someone could be you.

Good Drama Strategies:

- Save it for the school play!

- If you are exaggerating, be sure it is in good fun.

- If you are exaggerating to make someone look bad, that is bad. You are bad when you do that. Don't be a drama queen or a drama king. You might get crowned!

- Channel your love of drama into writing, DIY or maker-space activities, or some other creative outlet. I write kid's mysteries so I actually get paid to be dramatic! And don't believe all that drama on television talk shows. Trust me, a lot of that is made up—after all, no one wants to watch boring tv, right? But how those people act is not the real world.

- If you like drama, read history! No one can make up drama as incredible as things that have really happened in the past. Ask your school librarian/ media specialist for some ideas of really dramatic books, plays, or documentary videos.

- Don't put up with drama; if someone is trying to drama queen you, just walk away if they are having fun and you are not.

Don't Invite Trouble

It's good to stay OUT of trouble, not invite it into your life. Trouble will find you sometimes, anyway, but you don't have to invite it to your table.

Here are some trouble-free strategies:

- Pick good friends; they won't cause you as much trouble.

- Steer clear of troublemakers; you know who they are. Hanging out with troublemakers can get you into needless trouble.

- A lot of kids get in bad trouble not by doing anything wrong, but just by being an "accessory" or NOT doing something right. Don't put yourself in this position.

- *Run from trouble.* If you see a rumble ahead, a fight, a bad thing going down, just make a fast, quiet EXIT: Get out of there.

Anger Management

A lot of people, young and old, have a problem with anger management. What causes you to get angry? How do you avoid getting unnecessarily angry? If you get mad, do you feel compelled to get even? Are you slow to anger, or always on the verge of road rage?

Anger is a bad habit. Even if you have a reason to be angry, or have a chip on your shoulder, you can learn to manage your anger.

Anger can lead to bad things. Anger management is a good life skill.

Anger Management Strategies:

- Assume you'll get angry sometimes. Practice how you will respond. Make a good response a good habit. Don't give in to anger.

- Avoid angry people. They like to incite others to anger, then they sit back and laugh when you are the one who gets into trouble!

- Anger is often an over-reaction to something that is minor and passing. Learn to assess the situation and decide if it's even worth your while to get angry.

- *Don't jump to conclusions.* Maybe someone said something bad to you but meant it as a tease. Or were they just testing you? Don't fall for it.

- *Count to 10. Or 20. Or 100.* While you're counting, walk away, clean out your book bag, or check your texts—distract yourself from unnecessary anger.

- Deprive a person who wants to pick a fight. That may make them angry, but better them than you.

Anger can ruin your life. People can get carried away, or be determined to seek revenge. Later, no one may even recall what the argument was about, but there may still be a dead person.

Anger is childish. You are not a child. You would be angry if someone said you were. So, don't fall for anger. Be good. Smile.

Turn the Other Cheek

A good strategy to avoid getting sucked into bad stuff is just to turn the other cheek.

You have to learn that your ego is yours to manage. So what if you lose a little face by backing down, walking away, or turning the other cheek, if it saves you a world of hurt? Someone watching might even admire your guts to pass on this unnecessary opportunity to do bad or get in trouble.

Words hurt, yes, but you don't have to respond to every insult that comes your way. What someone wants is to incite you to anger. If you turn the other cheek, they may fume and taunt you, but really, you have just deprived them of the satisfaction of an angry reaction. *You win.*

Strategies:

- *Bide your time.* If you do not act upset, that may worry the other person. What do you know that they don't, they may wonder.

- Have someplace else to be and go there.

- *Act deaf.* What you didn't hear (even if you really did!) can't make you mad.

- *Act puzzled.* Nothing confuses the other person more than not being understood.

- *Agree!* That will shock someone! And, it may open a dialogue or discussion that even turns you into friends. People like to be heard. Adults who "argue" over important things like new laws, for example, usually do so in quiet, considerate conversations. If adults only yelled at each other, how would anyone ever agree? Let them get their side in; then, expect them to respect you sharing your side.

The Fruits of the Spirit

Focus on the fruits of the spirit. They are powerful tools in your goal to be good.

Love • Joy • Peace • Patience • Kindness • Goodness • Gentleness • Faithfulness • Self-Control

Let's look at them one at a time.

Love: If you love instead of hate, you will be good. When you see people on television showing hatred, don't you think that they look unhappy, like idiots, and you almost feel sorry for them? Love is so much better than hate.

Joy: If you focus on joyful things like friends and family, school, work, play—things that some kids don't have (and we grumble when we do!), you realize that you have plenty of reasons to be happy and to be good.

Peace: If you live in a democracy that is mostly peaceful, you have much more than most people on Earth. If you have a peaceful home, school, neighborhood, you have more than a lot of other kids do. Peace is a precious thing. Be good and be worthy of it.

Patience: Time has a way of evening things out. The ugly kid grows up to be beautiful, the poor one, rich, and the least likely to do well, well, they may end up in charge of everything! Don't expect everything instantly. If you bloom too soon, you may crash and burn later. Take your time. Live, grow, love, and be good. One day you'll realize all those corny things you hear like, "Life is the journey, not the destination" are so true.

Kindness: It costs nothing to be kind. If anyone has ever been kind to you even once, you know how special that is. Be kind, especially to other kids—you may have no real idea of what their life is actually like. They may need your kindness more than you will ever know. They may end up being good because you were good to them.

Goodness: We don't call it good for nothing. Be good when you can. Be good to your little sister or older brother, your parents, your teacher, your friends, the new kid in school, the old lady next door. Good is like a muscle; the more you exercise goodness, the easier, better, and stronger it gets.

Gentleness: Being gentle can mean all kinds of things. In a world where people do not seem to mind what ugly thing they say on the Internet, it's worth thinking about how not to be part of this problem. Yes, we may disagree, we may not like someone, we may have to critique someone. To correct them. Anyone can be wrong. In texts, you can read more into what someone says than they meant. So be gentle. It does not make you look weak; it makes you look mature.

Faithfulness: Be trustworthy; that's a good thing. Be loyal; that's how people know they can trust you. Have faith. Find friends you can trust and who will treat you right, no matter what.

Self-Control: This is a hard one. When you're still a kid, you're supposed to be immature. A little kid may have a tantrum because that's the only way they know how to get attention or to get their way. But no one wants to remain a little kid. Learn and practice self-control. There's nothing more unbecoming than an adult who can't control their emotions or actions. It's embarrassing to see them make a fool of themselves. Be mature. Have some self-control.

This Too Shall Pass

(and faster than you think!)

Kids are impatient. When you are five years old, you want to be ten. When you are ten, you can't wait to be a teen. What's your rush? It's a good thing to enjoy every age, each part of your life. (When you have a kid, that's what you'll tell them!)

Don't make life so hard for yourself that you wish it would go faster and you would get to a better place. Remember, you have NO idea what's coming next!

Instead, make each place better by being good. See the good in people. In places. Make good friends. Be a good friend. Be good to your parents; it's not easy raising kids in what often seems like a rotten apple world. Be good to your teacher—she's a mom, too, maybe. You don't know the problems she has. Even be good to the bad kid when you can. He or she may have a horrible home life, be scared to death, or have some other issue you don't know about. Just assume they want to be good, too, but may need a helping hand.

There are a lot of bad things in a kid's life. But acne goes away. Mean girls move on. Math will always be math; suck it up and do the best you can. Just assume that as soon as you get rid of one bad thing, another will pop up. But each good thing balances it out. Be good at what you're good at, even if it takes you some time to figure out what that is. In the meantime, be good at being good.

Good on Her!

A woman police officer heard about someone on her beat who desperately needed a new kidney. She got tested and was a match! She donated one of her kidneys to this young woman, who now can have a much better life.

Color is Only Skin Deep

As we see from the news, black cops shoot white people. White cops shoot blacks. We hear a lot about race and racism and racists. We see marching and protests.

But have you even seen a little white kid play with a little black kid? They are not thinking about the color of their skin. They are thinking about how they can climb up on a chair and get in the cookie jar!

While there are many reasons that people argue about race (and not just black and white), the truth is:

If a black person cuts his finger, his blood is red, not black. A white person skins her knee and she bleeds red, not white. A green person…well, we don't know what color alien blood is yet. But if a spaceship full of aliens showed up, I feel pretty sure that all people on Earth would suddenly feel like one color: Earthling color!

This is one time when kids can actually be the GOOD leaders in the world. The average classroom is full of all colors of kids. You work together, play together, do sports together, and are friends with one another. You often get along a lot better than adults do.

So when it comes to this race thing—Good grief, Be Good! Remember we are all the same color under our skin.

There's Always Someone Worse Off Than You Are

Feeling sorry for yourself? Thinking of all the reasons you may be entitled to be bad-to-the-bone? Well, there is always someone worse off than you are. *You know this is true.*

- There are refugees with no homes, often not even a country of their own.

- There are little kids with cancer; not all of them will be cured.

- Some kids have bad parents; orphans have no parents.

- Some kids are homeless.

- Some kids have one arm, eye, leg, or worse.

The list could go on and on. If you think you don't like your "bad stuff," just decide what "bad stuff" you would trade it for, and you might find you prefer to deal with the problems you have!

PART TWO: Tips, Tricks, and Secrets to Being a Good Kid

Note: If some of this seems a bit repetitious, it's because it's important and essential. There's a thing in writing called: "Tell em you're gonna tell em, tell em, tell em you told em!"

Don't Invite Trouble II

We run into enough trouble without inviting it to sit by us in school, follow us home, be our best (worse) friend. Develop a "sixth sense" of when a person, a party, or anything else does not seem or feel right—then avoid it. There are all kinds of ways to invite trouble. There are a lot of ways not to. Have some self-control. Try not to yell, argue, or automatically hit back. Practice anger management. If you want to hit something, take up baseball, archery, or kick-boxing. You get healthy and have fun doing those things; you can go to jail for hitting people. You see what I mean. It hurts when you get in trouble, especially if it is not really your fault. But it hurts really bad when you bring it on yourself. A lot of adults, who do not do well as adults, never figured out how not to invite trouble. Alcohol, drugs, bad friend choices, and more…they often make the same mistakes over and over. YOU are smarter and savvier than that!

Turn the Other Cheek: Often it's just easier to ignore someone who is bugging you—even if you are right and they are wrong. Walk off. Run away. Act deaf. Act dumb. Act confused. Nothing flummoxes a person with a big, bully mouth more than not being understood.

Ha, ha. Let them be the one who looks stupid, but don't stick around and gloat—go home. *Which leads me to…*

Turn the Other Butt Cheek: Sometimes, the best bet is to get the heck out of a situation. When you have the feeling that things could go from bad to worse, just leave. If mom or dad ever said, "Call me if…" this may be the time. Leave the building. Go for help. Skedaddle. While others are still there when the police come, the drugs go down, the lights go out—or whatever bad happens—you will be long gone. When you hear what happened later, you'll be glad you left!

Learn What the "Fruits of the Spirit" Are, Part II

This is a biblical thing, but you can be any religion or no religion. Most of us don't own these all the time, but they are a good shopping list for being good that you can aspire to. *Love, Joy, Peace, Patience, Kindness, Goodness, Gentleness, Faithfulness, and Self-Control.* Let's look at these again.

Love is good; you liked to be loved; you love some things. Love is not hate. So plant more love than hate. Practice love instead of bickering and arguing. You don't have to be ooey-gooey; just be nice.

Joy is good. Do more things that make you happy. Try to figure how to make things that you are not-so-crazy about to still make you happy. You might be surprised that you can feel joy about chores if you realize how much it helps your mom. Don't have so many rules. If you are a guy and you want to design a dress, design a dress. If you are a girl and you want to study astrophysics, go for it. If it makes you happy, it's probably the right thing for you. Some people never have much joy in their life because they did not seek it, want it, find it, and figure out how to get—and give—joy.

Peace is good. It's a noisy, often nasty world. You can find more peace alone, usually. Find a time each day just to be with yourself. A peaceful place helps, but it does not have to be a church or garden or forest. Peace is about inside your head. Even a little dose of peace each day helps you cope with the rest of the day.

Patience: You can often tell a kid from an adult by how much patience they have. (Not that all adults have that much patience, as you know!) But practicing patience is a good thing. You might find that while you are waiting on something or someone, something good happens. Many things can't be rushed anyway. Patience often pays off, and think how often you need someone to be patient with you.

Kindness: I am not sure we are born kind, but we can teach ourselves to be kind. Kind is good. It's just as easy to say please and thank you as not. It's nice to help people; they usually appreciate it. Kindness is often not about you. You are kind, but you are the one who feels the best about it. It makes you feel good. I once asked a father why he was so good to his sort of cantankerous mother. He said, "Because I thought it was so kind of her to take care of me when I was a baby and could do nothing for myself." I thought that was a pretty good answer. Kindness is a good habit; start young.

Goodness: Goodness is good. It is kindness but more. It is you being the best you can be. It is you doing more good things than bad. It is hard to explain, but being a good person feels good. Whether you are rich or poor, smart or not so smart, young or old, there is a special reward inside your head when you are good. I love to say, "He is such a good person." People almost always nod. How do we know? We just do; they just are. It's a good thing.

Gentleness: I love the idea of being gentle. You might think only a kindly, old granny is gentle. Nah. Sometimes, the biggest, baddest-looking halfback on a football team is gentle. Or the biker dude. Or the giant cop.

Gentle is what you do, how you are. It is not you being a sissy. It is you being big enough and brave enough to grab a kid's hand and walk her across the street. To say, "Hey, no problem!" (and mean it) to someone who made a mistake. To not laugh at someone just because others do. To shrug your shoulders and give a smile. To pat someone on the back. To thank a teacher.

Faithfulness: Wow, this is a hard one to explain. But you know who is faithful to you (if anyone is) and you really appreciate it. If someone can count on you, that's a big deal. Does anyone "have your back" or do you have theirs? There is a special bond when someone is faithful. It can be a mom, dad, kid, uncle, friend, teacher, or almost anyone. I had a sister-in-law who faithfully gave a quarter each day to a kid who had no lunch money. She never said, "Oh, sorry, I forgot." Faithful is more than good. That's how good faithfulness is.

Self-Control: Ouch, this is always a difficult one. We can control ourselves some of the time, most of the time, but probably not all of the time. Hey, we're human! Self-control takes practice to get good at it; starting young is a big help. Probably nothing makes your life better, easier, more successful, healthy, or happy than just plain old self-control. It's what YOU choose, not someone else. What YOU can do for YOU. Try it. Practice it. Perfect it. It's worth it. It's a good, good thing.

They call these "fruits," I think, because they are wonderful things. They say they are "of the spirit" because you cannot pick them up and hold them, buy them, or give them away. It is you doing good for good's sake. For you. For others. Most of the time, if not every time. It's like having a personal basket of really good things you can pick and choose from as you need them. And they never go away; they are always there for you—if you want and choose and use them.

This Too Shall Pass II

No, that's not a football term. It's a funny thing about being a kid. When you are six, you want to be seven. When you are ten, you want to be twelve. Long before you are a teen, you want to be a teen. As soon as you get to be a teen, you want to be twenty-one!

The grass always seems to be greener on the other side of a birthday. But anyone who is older can tell you that it is (or should be; I do understand it is not always) fun to be two, four, six, eight, ten, twelve, thirteen, eighteen, and to hurry things just deprives you of enjoying the age you are. Most of us want to be "older" because we think that is better. "If I were older, I would not be the little kid." "If I were bigger, I would not get picked on." "When I am a teenager I can do what I want to do."

But the truth is that every single year has benefits and problems. Growing up too fast, is, uh, well, growing up too fast. When I was a kid you had to wait to get a bike. Today, kids almost feel like they deserve a cell phone when they are born! (Or before?)

The problems you encounter at each age will pass. Your pesky older brother or sister may become your best friend. Benefits you might get when you are older may have responsibilities; when you are younger, you often get a free pass on those. So, be patient, relax, wait. Whatever is sort of an age-related pain will pass not only sooner than you think, but sooner than you might want it to.

Each age has good and bad. When you have kids, you will understand this. But when you are a kid, well, be a kid. One day you may look back fondly at the years you wanted to pass fast. I recall being nine and having no responsibilities and getting to read all I wanted, and just have fun playing. That passed. Why, I now wonder, was I in such a hurry for more homework, more chores, more problems—before I was ready for them? Be a good—even *great* first grader, fourth grader, eighth grader, twelfth grader. The rest is coming; don't rush it. Be good; be patient.

Color is Only Skin Deep II

One way to be good is to not be racist. I know that some parents are racist. When you live in their home, you pick up the wrong ideas. But even then, you might think, "Wow, my parents say this, but I have a lot of friends who are not the same color or background as me. What is right and what is wrong?" Your instincts will tell you what is good and right. I heard a great story of two girls, age nine, who told everyone they were twins. They loved each other. They spent all their time together. They dressed alike and liked the same things. One girl was black; one was white. In spite of their skin colors, they did not see how they could not be "twins" because they loved each other so much. No matter what skin color we have, our blood is red. We are all human beings. We want many of the same things. Honestly, kids have led the way in reducing racism. You sit in class with lots of different "flavors" of kids. You do not see skin color, you see friends. Good for you.

We Are All The Same Person!

Scientists say that the DNA of humans is 99.5% alike—for every person—so what are we so biased about? A .5% difference? Why?

There's Always Someone Worse Off II

It is good to remember this while you are whining or complaining about your own problems. Even as an adult, I am amazed at how some people—kids of all ages, and adults—can lose eyes, arms, legs, parents, homes, and more—yet still be positive and optimistic. They inspire me. I do not know them but I love them and admire them and wish them the very best in life. I once created a game called "Meet in the Middle" to teach my own kids how to understand how good they had it, even when they were poor, almost homeless, had divorced parents, and other problems. I reminded them they were American, they had a mom and a dad, they had a home to live in, they got to go to school, and much more. Over time, they began to see what I meant. They had friends who died or who had brothers or sisters who died. They knew homeless people. They still would whine, but not as much. No matter how bad off you are, you can easily find someone who has it much worse. Being grateful for your own blessings is a good thing. Time passes and sometimes the poor kid gets rich. The kid who lost both legs to cancer wins a gold medal in the Paralympic Games. Anything can happen. Be patient. Be good. Work hard. Wait and see. You might be surprised!

Plan, But Don't Plan

One thing that adults are not very good about is planning. Oh, they plan. But they just assume everything will work out how they planned it. I have not noticed life being so neat and tidy as that! Planning is good. But also watch for what you *did not* plan. If you don't get in the college of your choice, it may be that you end up doing something much better. Plan, but be open to opportunities and possibilities that you never planned on. Be flexible. I never really believed that I could make my living as a writer, so I did not plan to do so. However, making a living as a writer is all I have ever done in my career. I could not have planned it better!

Worry, But Don't Worry

When I was a kid we had a family friend who was an undertaker. He buried the dead. Even as a kid, when he told me, "It's never what you think!" I knew he meant that no one could predict how they might die. You can worry about a gazillion things: Am I smart enough, pretty enough, strong enough? Will I do this right or that wrong? What if I don't get in the school I want, or meet the person I want? Worry, worry, worry all you want to, but you will probably worry about things that never affect you. A good strategy to be good is to worry as little as possible. Instead, have faith that things will work out like they are supposed to, as long as you just keep working and plugging ahead. You might have a good idea, a great plan, but God may have a better idea and a better plan!

GIGO, Garbage In/Garbage Out

This is a technology term. If you enter crappy data into your computer database, well, do not expect to get any better info out of it! The same is true in life. Shovel bad stuff into your life—bad thoughts, bad actions, bad people, bad habits—and only bad can come out of that. But put good thoughts, good habits, good food, good exercise, good fun, good friends, and more good things, into your day, your mind, and your thinking, then when you need an idea, a cheer-up, a plan, good things will happen. So, I guess that's still GIGO, only Good In/Good Out!

Read Bios

You may or may not like to read. You probably have to read for school, and for sure you will have to read for work one day. One really good thing to read is biographies of good people. I don't mean long, boring books about old people or dead people (although some of them are definitely worth reading about), but very short bios of cool, good people who may have overcome a lot of incredible obstacles to have a great life. As a writer, I have written a lot of biographies. I always try to tell what the person did as a kid your age, not just after they were famous. I am always so surprised that almost every single person that I have written about had a pretty sorry childhood or teen years. They were often considered dumb or just inept at anything they tried.

Even Milton Hershey, who was a really good man and who invented milk chocolate (Thank you, Milt!), built a town and factory to give jobs to people during the Great Depression, started a school, and built an orphanage for kids with no families. When he was a teen and young adult, there was just one thing he was unable to do, and that was to make candy! Yep, he was a candy klutz. But he thought good thoughts.

One day, he thought about all the cows on the hillsides in Pennsylvania. And then he had the idea that maybe adding milk to chocolate (which tasted pretty yucky back then) might make it taste really good. (You think?) The *Hershey Bar* was born and so was a chocolate legend—and a good boy went on to be a great man.

Bios like that are fun to read! You learn something, for sure. If they can do that, well, what might you be able to do good and worthy? What you *can't* do has NOTHING to do with what you *can* do. And mistakes and missteps often lead to the best ideas, decisions, and life ever. (Maybe that's why we have to make them!) Your teacher or librarian will be THRILLED to point out some biography series that you might enjoy. After all, everyone famous has one (a bio, that is), and that includes football quarterbacks, race car drivers, tech geeks, fashion designers, and more.

Honestly, nothing is more impressive, helpful, and inspiring than to read how other people became good in spite of bad things and mistakes and obstacles ranging from blindness to failing school, to just about any bad thing you can think of—and many astounding things that you can't! One day, some kid may read your *Bio of a Good Kid* and go, "WOOOOOW!"

Seek and Find/Hide and Seek

A lot of kids waste a lot of time on social media. Social media is great, but you can watch life, or live it. Spend some of your time seeking ideas and info and people online who actually teach you something. You will find that there are amazing people and projects going on all the time.

Just the other day, I watched a man who was so excited because he had figured out how to make spider web! Only spiders can make a web, which is a miracle kind of substance. But he researched and figured out how to brew yeast and other things that would make a spider web. Then he extruded it and created a web on a roll and is now making miracle products out of it. Products like clothing for soldiers that will not burn. Now, I like to keep up with my friends on Facebook, and to watch cute puppy videos, Instagram with my grandkids, and all that. But nothing gives me cold chills and makes me smile like a spider-web-beer-brewing genius scientist. I want some of the socks he makes that will never have any holes in them!

What about "Hide and Seek?" You don't always have to share everything, you know. If you want to research,

Google, read up on good things that others might make fun of, then just hide-out on your own and seek this information. No one thought my being a writer was possible or a good idea, so I just worked on my writing in secret. I had a good time doing that. It was not a waste of time, but a big head start on my career. Your time is your own (well, mostly), so do a good job of managing the free time you have and you might look back and think it was the best time you ever spent!

A Good Skill Is a Good Thing

I admire all kinds of workers. Have you ever watched a floor-cleaner tackle a gym floor all scuffed up with heel prints and sticky with gum? That floor looks so trashed! But a person with the know-how and skill to transform it back into the shiny marvel of a floor in time for the next game possesses a remarkable (and a marketable!) skill.

It takes a lot of unique skills to make the world go around. People who are good at their skills are good people. We often admire doctors, scientists, tech gurus, billionaire business entrepreneurs, and others, and rightly so. But I had an uncle who could cook great food in giant quantities for a squadron of soldiers. I never understood how he did that; those giant pots were intimidating!

I see people all the time who have awesome skills. Even one bona-fide (real thing you can do) skill is a good thing. Most people love their skills. I would if I could build a skyscraper or a bridge, and so many other things. A great actor, singer, or teacher, is easy to admire. But I also greatly admire garbage collectors. Do you know how hard a job that is? Do you realize the organization, time management, strength, and endurance it takes to get this job done? Oh, yeah, and garbage collectors can make good money. It's a team effort and they are proud of what they do. Get a skill. Get a good skill. Polish that skill and take pride in it. A good skill is a good thing.

Why You Go to School

You go to school to learn. No matter what you learn, you can build on that learning. The harder you work at school, the smarter you will be. This comes in handy when you begin to decide what job you might want to have in life. No matter what the job is, it is best to be good at it. We do not want bad doctors, we want good doctors. We do not want bad bridge builders, we want good bridge builders.

You go to school to learn, even if you are not too excited about school. Once you learn what you love, you usually love to learn more about that subject. You learn skills. More importantly, you begin to see why being GOOD is so important. It is the GOOD people of the world who make sure that our roads and cars are safe, that our food is healthy, that we stay well, that a roller coaster does not run off its tracks, that the rocket goes up, not down, and so much more.

We take for granted all the GOOD things that happen each day. That's because they work so good. (Uh, did your toilet flush this morning? Good on the plumber!) GOOD people make the Internet work, predict the weather, the church stay warm in the winter, make sure the hamburgers come hot off the grill, and lots of other things. You go to school to get GOOD at something. The something you may learn to be best at is being you!

Your Parents Don't Know Everything (But Don't Tell Them That!)

I do not say this to "diss" your parents, trust me. Parents know a lot. Some parents are older and wiser. Some are still learning. Some, as we know, are total deadbeats. But to be a good kid, you will have to get good at discerning when to listen to adults, and when not to.

Wisdom Wow

Even kids can be wise for their age. A good trait is to learn to be the voice of reason, to be silent when that's the best bet, and to speak up when you know what you are talking about. When I was a kid, I wanted to be wise, but figured that I was too young to know what wisdom was. But a lot of time, I was wise. That surprised me. Wisdom was a good thing to learn, experience, and practice when I got the chance.

Humility

It is good to be humble. Kids (and adults) who brag on themselves, think they know everything, worry about who has the most, the biggest, etc. usually pretty much make fools of themselves. One of my favorite kids (now she is a young adult) is Malala Yousafzai. She is the young Muslim girl who wanted all girls in her country to go to school. She was shot in the head for speaking out. Miraculously, she recovered—won a Nobel Peace Prize!—and continues her fight for educational justice for girls. She has even spoken at the United Nations. She is soft-spoken with a beautiful smile. She could not be more humble, even though she has much to be proud of. Humility is a good thing.

ET, The Extraterrestrial

Remember what he said? *"Beeee gooood."* Do you think if a real alien came to visit Earth it might offer that advice to us? (Who knows, we may find out one day!) Be Good is good advice. When you have the chance, dance, goes one country music song. When you have the choice, Be Good. It's not hard. It's easy. It's a habit. Some good is made up of such simple things: a smile; a kind word; a thank you; helping out.

Yoda

Another wise alien was Yoda. He might say, "Behave bad, do not you." More good advice!

Superman, Wonder Woman, and Other Superheroes

You meet them every day. Some are firefighters; others may be emergency room nurses. (For me, it's the guy who comes to unstop my toilet!) Heroes are good. They are usually humble. While in the movies, most wear red capes or other superhero clothing. In real life a superhero might wear muddy boots or no make-up. But we each have an invisible red cape. As we go about our day, we can sometimes be a superhero just by being good.

The Three Amigos

My grandson, Grant, had two good friends, Michael and Weng-Ho. I called them the three amigos. They were really good boys. Oh, they were boys, and got dirty and ran and had fun, but what amazed me is how good they were to each other. They mostly got along, took turns, shared, and stayed friends until they were adults. When I saw all three of them together, I often thought, "These boys are so good that I would have any of them for my grandkid." In fact, when I squinted, I thought, "In some ways they are all the same person—just a good kid."

The truth is that I think we are all the same person. We each have good and not so good in us. We each are children of God. We each are made up of the same stuff, no matter what the color of our skin or what language we speak.

As you get older, you might find that you feel the same way. And so being good should not be dependent on who YOU are with or what THEY do. Sometimes you will do the right thing, and sometimes, you may not. But that is true of the other person too.

We are each on a path from birth to death, and we each have different backgrounds, places we live, and life goals. But really, we are each a human being, hopefully one trying to be as good as we can. I always say, "The person you may not want to sit next to on a bus may turn out to be an EMT who gives you CPR and saves your life!" Maybe we should strive to be a gazillion amigos, each with our arm around the other. Being good is easier when we do it together.

Be a Friend to Have a Friend

I know that sounds old-fashioned and corny, but it is true. A good person is a good friend. But you may not always know who is your good friend until they show up! A boy I know got on drugs and drinking and smoking. He was not healthy; he was sick. He would not change or get help or listen to anyone. His parents were shocked when the least likely "friend" (another boy on drugs) called them and asked if he could try to help. (He needed help himself, but he wanted to help his friend.) He did! Now that's a good friend!

If You Ever Read Ann Landers

I know you did not; you are too young. There was a woman called "Dear Ann," and that was the name of her newspaper column. Millions of people read it every day. It was an advice column. Ann had good advice. You could go to work and overhear people arguing whether her advice to someone who had written in the day before was good or bad. Later, Ann's daughter (also called Ann) took over the column. She had good advice, too. By that time, it covered things like bullying, social media, and other concerns we have today.

If you need advice, ask someone. They may be able to help you. If you get asked for advice, try to give good advice. I loved "Dear Ann" because she often said simple, logical things, like "Life is for the living." She made you want to get up, get dressed, do something, be good. She (and her daughter) listened, had a lot of wisdom, and shared it well. They were good people.

Get Up, Get Dressed, Get Going

This is good advice for anyone. You can sit and sulk, procrastinate or think, "Oh, woe is me." It's always a good idea to get a good night's sleep. Then in the morning, get the heck up! Get dressed! And get going! For you, that may be to the gym, or early to school, or even just to the kitchen for a healthy breakfast, or to help your mom. Good things happen when you get up, get dressed, and get going. I don't know why that is, but when I get up, get cute, and get outta there, the world seems to meet me. If a friend asks, "Do you want to go to __________?" I am ready already! If someone needs my help, I am prepared. If I have a class, I am the first one there with time to spare, get the best seat, schmooze the teacher, and have time for a snack. I like good things to happen, but they seem to happen more often when I rise and shine, have something ready to wear, a plan, and get going. Try it.

Role Model

Hey, that's you! Somebody's gotta be a good role model, it might as well be you. People may look up to you. They may wish they were you. Younger kids are watching. So are parents, teachers, coaches, and others. You don't have to do anything special, but being good is a good start. This book is full of good stuff; pick a few. Who are your role models? Odds are they are not the slouches, or those always in trouble. The best thing is that you are not playing a role, you are just being you—the YOU that you worked hard to become.

The Value of Reading

When I was a kid, I read everything. Everything that was: a) close up; or b) in big print. I had terrible eyesight from being born prematurely. But I LOVED books, not just for what they said, but as objects. I loved the way they felt and smelled, and, yes, tasted. (Well, maybe I was a weird kid?) I loved picture books. At least they were oversized and had big type and big pictures. If I could not read the words, I would make up stories to go with the illustrations.

After I spent all of first grade in Reading Group, I finally (barely) learned to read the giant *Dick and Jane* book. After that, I spent as much time reading as I could, especially in the summertime. Back then, librarians did not care how many books you checked out or whether they were from the juvenile or adult section. So, after I read all the books in the kids' section, I started on the adult books. I really liked fairy tales and National Geographic books with naked natives in them! Reading was not a chore; it was fun. I was so engaged in my reading that I often would not even speak to my family; I was too busy (for example) secretly chewing on imaginary seal skin, like the mother in the book about Eskimos that I was reading. (You can't chew seal and talk at the same time!) Since no one cared what I read, I read all kinds of things, learned all kinds of things, and learned to love all kinds of things. Mummies, dinosaurs, werewolves, tornadoes, and most anything else scary and creepy and hard-to-believe were my favorite things to read about.

I grew up, became a writer, and guess what I wrote about? You guessed it! Hurricanes and vampires, and anything weird and mysterious. I make a living doing this! So, my point is, reading is good. Reading the Bible is good. But reading anything is good. Once, a very smart kid asked me (very suspiciously, like I was cheating or something), "Ms. Marsh, how do you know so much stuff?" I waited a minute and then got right in his face and said, "I READ!" I have no idea why that answer would surprise anyone.

If you want to learn how to be a good kid, read. So many characters (real and imaginary) have awful times in books. Many of these books are true. And how they overcome, end up helping others, being good people, and living amazing lives is just awesome. Reading is just about the goodest thing I know!

Why Be Good?

You have a purpose! You may not know what it is yet… but what a waste to waste any of your life, to later find out that you have a great purpose that you really want to pursue. Hang in there! Life can be good, even great! Your purpose is important. You could end up changing the world. So be good, press on, and when you finally figure out your purpose, you will be so glad you did!

What Separates the Men from the Boys and the Women from the Girls?

We often admire the rich and the famous, or the strong and the powerful. Not me. I admire real men, even if they are only six years old. Have you ever seen a little boy fight cancer? He is more manly than many grown men. Of course a man who is an EMS and will breathe into anyone's mouth to save a life is a "real man" too, in my book.

Sometimes we girls rave over who is the cutest, the best-dressed, the sexiest, the social media butterfly. But a girl who is a woman can often be found taking care of her younger brothers and sisters while her mother works three jobs. And a grown woman who helps kids with learning disabilities is sort of a superhero! So, it's not about age. It's about being a good person no matter what your age.

You can always make money. You can become famous (and not like it!) You can be rich and famous and very unhappy. But it's hard to meet a truly good person who is miserable, alone, lonely, unhappy, or bored.

I talked about biographies earlier. My favorite bios are of people who have really hard, dangerous, nasty jobs but love them so much and are so good at them, that they are not just happy, but utterly happy! Now that's the kind of "good" that is just plain great!

Politeness

I just heard a cute story. This girl had a date. The date picked her up and sat and sat in the car waiting for her. After a long time, he realized that she was standing by the passenger door of his car…waiting for him to open the door for her! The girl's father, a gentleman, had taught her that good guys always open the door for a woman. Now, maybe that sounds old-fashioned, but guess what? It's not! The guy finally hopped out and opened her door. He never forgot again. And, of course, she said yes when he asked her to marry him! Being polite is a good thing to do. It takes almost no time and costs no money. No one should ever refuse politeness or make fun of it. Politeness is like a gift you did not ask for, may not deserve, but that makes you feel happy and appreciated. You are welcome for this advice. Thank you for listening.

Create Your Own Sense of Beautiful

Nothing helps you be good more than just being yourself. Don't fall into the trap of trying to be like others. I once knew a man who was a reporter. He died young. One of his last newspaper columns talked about "Create Your Own Sense of Beautiful." He loved that some poor (even homeless) people he saw downtown where he worked created their own version of beauty that suited them. There was a girl who always wore a red hat. There was a man who decorated a little Christmas tree at his "homeless" spot. As the reporter was dying, he said he had learned that only YOU can create what seems beautiful to you in life. It's a good habit to get into when you are young. Just because everyone else is doing X or wearing Y, does not mean you have to.

Doing your own original thing that makes you happy is a lot more fun. It always will be. That's good.

Thank You Cards

A really easy way to be good is to buy (or even better, make) some thank you cards. Once my granddaughter stenciled suns and rainbows on paper and folded them into thank you note cards. She would send them to me or anyone she wanted to thank for something. Not only was this a good thing, it made people smile and it made people remember her. If I wanted to give someone a job, and I recalled that once they sent me a thank you card, they would go to the head of the line. Why? Because I would know that they were a good, caring person who would always take the time to do the right thing. Good to know, don't you think?

There's (Still) Always Someone Worse Off

Look how good some kids are who have terrible problems: no parents; one parent; abuse; homelessness; sickness; mental issues; and much more. I have found that most kids are just naturally good. But when you find yourself choosing bad things, ways, words, friends, etc., then stop and think, "What if I had ________?" and realize that you are lucky enough to choose to be good. Yes, everyone has problems, often really bad ones, but if everyone wrote down their serious problem and put it on a table and you read them all and could pick any one, you probably would pick the one you have!

What Are Kids Concerned About Today?

A School Library Journal poll found the major concerns were: bullying, cyberbullying, suicide, opiod abuse, gender identity, school safety, self-image, sexual consent… and that was just the top of the list. What concerns you today?

Don't Stand at the End with Empty Hands

A good way to look at things is to think, "Well, what will I have at the end of this?" The end could be the end of a day, the end of an argument, the end of a party, or, yes, the end of your life. Things don't really need to be so dramatic, you know. Don't let drama queens or bullies make you think that. That's just fake excitement. If you make good choices, at the end of the day you might be worn out from all you had to do and get a good night's sleep. At the end of an argument, if you listened to the other person, you might end up with a new friend instead of an enemy. At the end of a party, you might end up alive, if you did not drink and drive (or ride with someone who did). Same goes for drugs. And lots of other things. Where do you want to end up at the "end?" In the next grade? With the job you wanted? Passing the test? Not in the principal's office? That's the kind of good planning that pays off!

Self-Control II

You know what that is. It's the ability to choose what your brain, your eyes, your mouth, your arms, hands, legs, and more will and won't do. As a little kid, you might bite someone. (And they just might bite you back!) You may not have chosen to do that, you just did it. Maybe it looked like fun, maybe you were hungry, maybe you were mad. But you're not a little kid anymore.

Most of the time you can perfectly well choose not to yell or scream. To say nice words (or keep your mouth shut!) instead of saying something mean or hateful. You can usually choose what to look at and control how you look at another person. You can sure decide whether—or not—to ball up your fist and slug someone, or to just give them a pat on the back. To kick a shin or a soccer ball. Every day is full of choices to just react or to practice self-control. Self-control is a good thing. Often the person it's best for is YOU!

Patience II

Most people have little patience. That's too bad; patience is a good thing. Even adults can be so impatient, don't you think? A lot of times, if you just WAIT to speak, to argue, to say the first thing that comes out of your mouth, to react, to hit back, to have road rage (well that would be adults), then you find the problem or issue just sort of blows away. Count to ten. Count to twenty. Count to one hundred. Just wait. Wait and see. Problem? What problem? "Wow," you might say, "I'm glad I waited!"

Adults Are Idiots?

I know, sometimes you may wonder why YOU have to behave decently when you see adults act like big babies, bullies, or buttheads. (Yeah, I said buttheads in a kid's book; guess I have no self-control!) But you know what

I mean. Sometimes when I see people acting badly, it just makes me want to be better. There's nothing like watching someone make a fool of themselves—especially an adult acting like a kid!—to make you see why a lot of the things in this book are good ideas.

Sure, everyone gets angry sometimes, or forgets to be polite. But when you have road rage, or walk right by a person who needs help, or speak ugly to an old lady, and a lot of other things, it's just so unnecessary. Yes, some people have mental problems, or maybe they never got to read a book like this, or perhaps people have been cruel to them. All I know is that it is just as fast, easy, and safer to be good than to be bad. I think being bad must get sort of boring. And you sure can't make many friends! Bad is a bad habit. Good takes practice. We sure need good to outweigh bad in our homes, lives, and personal choices. Really, you don't want to look and act like an idiot when you grow up, do you? And what is "grown up" anyway? Some kids act a lot better than adults, I think.

Bolt Hole

One good way to be good is just to hunker down or get away when you are feeling mean, spiteful, hateful, or some other negative emotion. Instead of taking your bad mood out on your mother or brother, go take a nap, sit in the sun (with sunscreen on!), or throw a baseball. Get away to your bolt hole, a private place or time to clear your head and calm down. Give yourself a break. Everyone deserves a time out when they feel ornery. We all have days like that, or get our feelings hurt, or just feel bad and out of sorts. It's bad to inflict all that on someone else. Go do something else instead and you might find that before you know it, you feel better, like yourself, and are back to being in a good mood again. My calm down place is a hammock or a bicycle seat, or the beach. But I'll also settle for a good book. (Or some ice cream, when I feel like screaming.)

Safety Valves

Like a bolt hole, having some surefire ways to not be lured into being bad is something to think about ahead of time. Some kid might think, "Well, I sure would like to have a tantrum, but then I'll just get stuck in time out." Or, "I really want to smack that girl, but I'll just end up in the principal's office." A safety valve might be a sport—go play and take out your frustrations on that tennis ball, golf ball, soccer ball, or punching bag. A safety valve might be a place where you can be alone. I guess everyone needs a tree house! Another kind of safety valve can be a friend who will listen to you and let you vent your frustrations. They may not agree, but they will listen and let you blow off steam. Again, my safety valve is a good book where I can soon forget what I was so upset about. A video game would work, too. Or doing something for someone else instead of feeling so sorry for yourself. Think of five safety valves and be able to tap the fingers on one hand to bring them to mind when you need them. (Trust me, you'll need them!)

Success Stories

I love "good people" success stories! One thing is often certain, a lot of bad things happened before the success. So how do kids who have it really bad end up being so good, positive, and successful? I think it comes with a lot of pain and a lot of practice. Frankly, I can't imagine losing my arms and legs and then going on to become a happy, successful, good person. But I know people who have done this. Or been orphans, never adopted, lived in many foster homes, and then when they turned eighteen, sent out to live on their own. How are they supposed to end up good? Just learning what some kids have to go through makes you more accepting of your own problems. Of whatever you think is in the way of you being good. And makes you more forgiving and accepting of kids having hard times and taking it out on you. There are a lot of ways to end up a winner, but it often starts with bad stuff. One good thing can make all the difference in the world! Maybe YOU can be that one good thing!

What About Faith?

It never hurts (and often helps) to believe in something. That may be God, Jesus, Buddha, Allah, or something else. If you go to church, synagogue, or some other organized religious place, then that's probably good. I love to visit my grandkids' church. It has a great band, a cool light show each week, a young minister who wears jeans, and donuts to eat! What I like best is that everyone is nice and friendly. Everyone feels included. It's a place where you might get help or advice, even as a kid. And kids play a big role in the church. So seek faith, have faith, or at least think about faith. I believe in something—I believe in you!

Zombie—Not!

Being a zombie is not a good idea. It is not really so cool to just zone out, stay cooped up in your room, tune out the world. It really isn't! A good thing is to tune in—find out what is going on and be part of the solution, not part of the problem. Don't sleep your life away. Don't act as if the world can get by without you. It can't!

You can be quiet. You can be shy. You can listen instead of speak. (That's often a very good idea; more people should try it!) But don't be a zombie because you think you are cool, or you are afraid, or for any other reason.

This crazy, often RAW (Rotten Apple World) needs you! It needs you now. It needs you as a kid. And it will need you as an adult.

I think the world is getting better. What usually makes the world better is good young people who come along just in the nick of time with good ideas. Some of those people fought in World War II and saved the world. Others sent (or flew in) rockets into space when that was new and scary and dangerous. Some invented great things to help save lives, like organ transplants.

What will YOU do when you grow up? Who knows? But "the walking dead" never get very far very fast. There is a worse thing than being bad and that's being dead when you are still alive. Life is too good to waste, so don't!

Phooey with Failure

One thing we don't seem to teach kids at school or at home is that failure is good! Really? Yep! Where would most famous people be if they had not failed along the way? A mistake just shows you that one thing did not work that way at that time. What if Einstein, Edison, and other scientists and inventors gave up because they failed? Oops! We might not have computers, space ships, or Disney World. Oh, dear. It's a good idea to keep at *it*, whatever *it* is. If *it* was easy, everybody would do *it*. But maybe *it* is for you to keep trying until you get *it* right!

Money

Just one good word about money—learn about it. The more you know, the more you can become a good money maker and money manager. My kids pretty much stayed out of trouble because they did not have much time to get into any—they were working. My kids had chores. They were always busy with a newspaper route, babysitting, cutting grass, or doing office work for me. If you save more than you spend, you will have money for stuff you want. You won't have to use credit cards or borrow money for most things. (Now some people will say that is not true, but I know that it is!) Good money management is for kids as well as adults. And you CAN work your way through college and end up with no debt!

Don't think you HAVE to go to college to be successful.

Going to college, voc ed school, tech college, online learning, etc. are all good, but you can also not go to college and end up successful. Once I spoke at a high school. One kid asked me, "Ms. Marsh, where did Steve Jobs, Michael Dell and Bill Gates graduate from college?" Now these are 3 of the richest and most successful men in the world. BUT they all dropped out of college! Each went "to their garage" (so to speak, or for real) and invented something that went on to change the world.

PART THREE: What About Really Rotten Stuff?

Hmm, as I was writing this book, I wondered how to be sure it was not dated. After all, every day's news headlines seem to bring more Rotten Apple World stuff.

The latest RAW stuff (to me):

- Increased drug use, overdose, and death.
- Increased suicide, often as a result of depression, bullying, or other things related to Internet activity.
- And tragic school shootings.

Let's talk about these a bit.

Drug use: There are good things and bad things. But using drugs is just a dangerous thing. It is not smart or cool. It is just plain dangerous. Many kids have used drugs just one time and died. The "drugs" you might take are not like the medicine you take for an illness. Drugs can be really, really bad. They may not even be the kind of drugs you think. Someone may have messed with them and made them more dangerous. They may be too powerful for your system. A good thing is not to try drugs, sell them, buy them, be around people who use them, or encourage others to use them. And this advice is for adults, too, so it sure is good advice for kids, kid!

Depression and suicide. There are some things that I cannot cover in this book. If adults need help, then kids sure need help. A good strategy is that if you feel down and depressed, and certainly if you have any thoughts of killing yourself, then get help. A parent, a friend's parent, a teacher, a school counselor, a minister—almost anyone will stop and help a kid who says they feel this way. It is not something to be ashamed of, or to worry about all by yourself. Get help! Don't let something that can be cured/fixed ruin your life. We need you!

This dadgum school shooting business. It makes me mad, it really does. Kids are citizens, too. You deserve to go to school and be safe. I think that it is sad that some adults, and some younger-than-adults are so disturbed that they choose shooting as an outlet for their frustrations. (We all wish that they had sought help or that someone had helped them.)

I think it's pretty amazing that after the school shooting in Florida, kids were really angry. You go to school to learn how to be a good citizen. And I think that the kids who spoke up about how they felt were being good citizens. I think adults should listen. In the meantime, just be good. It really isn't a rotten apple world; there are just some bad apples in the human barrel. Let's be good and help one another.

WHAT WOULD YOU BE WILLING TO SEEK HELP FOR?

WHAT WOULD YOU BE WILLING TO DO TO HELP SOMEONE WHO NEEDED HELP?

WHAT WOULD YOU STAND UP, MARCH, OR PEACEFULLY PROTEST ABOUT?

THE MOST IMPORTANT TWO PAGES IN THIS BOOK

When you feel overwhelmed, ask for help. If you have really bad thoughts that make you feel you are a danger to yourself, or to others, ask for help right away! You do not have to suffer alone. There is help. It may not always be instant, and it may not be from the first person you ask. Just keep asking. It can be a friend, family friend, parent, classmate, teacher, teacher's aide, principal, counselor, minister, rabbi, or almost anyone else.

It might be a good thing to go ahead and sort of look around and think, "If I ever felt weird or had a problem, who could I trust to listen and help?" Have a couple of "go to" people in mind. It's not hard to develop a sixth sense of who is a good person, a person who could help when help is needed. If you get really desperate, go to an Emergency Room or a fire station; they are used to all kinds of situations—physical and mental. They will listen and they will help.

And everyone should keep an eye open for the kid who might need help, who is lonesome, hurting, left out, even scared or scary. We are our brothers' and sisters' keepers. I hate to read in the newspapers, "I wish I'd known he needed help." Or, "I thought she might need a friend." When your conscience tells you something, listen and act. None of us ever knows when we will be the helper or the helped.

HAVE YOU EVER MET SOMEONE WHO ASKED YOU FOR HELP?

HAVE YOU EVER ASKED SOMEONE IF THEY NEEDED OR WANTED HELP?

HAVE YOU EVER TOLD AN ADULT THAT YOU THOUGHT A CERTAIN PERSON NEEDED HELP?

THE BEST TWO PAGES IN THIS BOOK

Not only is there HELP for what ails you, there is HOPE.

Even if you do the bad thing, even the worse thing, there are still people in this world who are there to help you. Alas, it may be a lawyer, a doctor, a judge, even a police officer. They have seen it all. You may be in Big Trouble, but even kids in Big Trouble are entitled to help. Often, I hate to say, getting in trouble is the first step on the road to getting help, healing, and getting better. It may not be fun or pretty; in fact, it may be pretty awful. But you can heal, and move on.

One time, my husband (who had Parkinson's disease) fell down. He had fallen down a lot that day. He had some mental issues and he had the physical issues of the disease, and he was really, really stubborn! So when he fell on the carpet, I was so tired of seeing him fall and risking breaking a hip (or worse) that I let him stay there. He could not get up on his own.

My grandson, Grant, came in and saw this; he was upset. "Why don't you get Papa up?!" he asked. "Because,"

I said, "now that he is down, he can no longer fall. I think he just needs to lay there a bit and rest and calm down." That's what my sweet husband did; and then we helped him up.

When you hit rock bottom, there is no farther down to go, so the only way is up.

There is always help and always hope, so never forget that. Some of the greatest success stories come from people (of all ages) who fell the farthest. But, uh, do try to avoid that…

HAVE YOU EVER FALLEN DOWN?

HAS ANYONE EVER HELPED YOU UP?

HAVE YOU EVER HELPED SOMEONE ELSE UP?

THE SCARIEST PAGES IN THIS BOOK

(Oh, I am in for it now with your parents just for bringing this subject up, but, hey, I'm here to help YOU!)

SEX

I have written a lot of sex education books. Some of them have funny titles. But there is nothing funny, or right, about sex when YOU know that whatever is going on is wrong. You must learn to speak up!

As you may know, there is the terrible news story about the Olympic gymnasts who were sexually abused over several years by someone who was supposed to be taking care of them. (He is now in jail for life.) I don't care if it is a kid your age (or even younger), an older kid, a family "friend," an adult of any kind, or even someone you think might not ever do such things (like a doctor), trust your instincts. If it is wrong, tell someone!

I'm sorry it has to be your problem to start solving, that YOU have to tell, but often that is the only way a solution begins to happen. If the first person does not believe you, go to the next person. (Don't forget to identify a few people you think you can trust ahead of time.)

Yes, there are kids who lie about such things, or maybe who imagine such things. But that is rare. What is not so rare are kids who are abused or molested. NOPE! We are NOT having that. Even though I'm not going into a lot of specifics, you know that your body is YOUR body. Don't be bullied or threatened into silence. TELL. It never gets better, but it can get worse. So tell as soon as something is going on and do not let up until you get help. In a desperate situation, go to the ER or the fire station. They will understand. They will not even be surprised. They will help.

And this applies to things that are not physical abuse. Only now are we beginning to accept that some kids are born with different sexualities. Sometimes, adults don't even want to think about this, much less talk about it. But that is the adults' problem. Don't let it be your problem. YOU are entitled to be YOU. Go to those trusted people and ask for help and advice.

You know, a librarian is always a good helper. She can guide you to good books that may help you understand better what might be happening to you. Look out for yourself, and look out for others. As I said, we are all in this together.

We CAN get the rotten apples out of the world barrel. Let's not let them go from kid to kid to kid because no one tells on them.

Kathy's Comment

Unfortunately, I know personally of a few children who are in challenging circumstances with adults, usually parents, who are setting bad examples–domestic fights, drinking, encouraging them to lie, etc. Having another adult voice that offers positive messages and sound advice can mean so much for a kid's future. If they don't see a possible alternative to the bad stuff, they can't choose the good stuff!

Boyfriends & Girlfriends

It's bound to happen! Have fun. Here are tips to help you have fun. If you are not having fun, then this is not the person for you. You don't want or need a rotten apple boyfriend or girlfriend.

- Don't make fun of or embarrass each other.
- Support each others' goals; don't put each other down.
- Don't intimidate or threaten.
- If someone says, "You are nothing without me," don't believe them.
- No one is jealous of someone because they "love them so much."
- Don't put up with any physical abuse, ever.
- Don't stick around if your person uses drugs or tries to get you to.

- Don't be pressured into sex you are not ready for or do not want.

- Don't let anyone prevent you from being with your other friends.

- Don't make everything the other person's fault.

- Text for fun, not for keeping an eye on your person!

Remember, it's supposed to be a boy "friend" or a girl "friend," so if it's not feeling friendly, it's not for you!

Internet Etiquette

Look, you gotta have some smarts when it comes to online communication. No matter if that is email, Facebook, Instagram, or new things that come up, watch what you say! The world is listening—really!

- Keep in mind that talking face-to-face is the best bet.

- Always be respectful. In person, someone can tell by your face that you are teasing, but online words can sound mean.

- Never be mean.

- Watch your language. Everything you say online will be there forever. Think if you want your grandkids to read (or see) certain things.

- Watch your photos. They never go away! There is no eraser on the Internet!

- Don't hurt anyone's feelings. You may feel different tomorrow, but the hateful words will still be there, for all to see.

- Right now, we see a backlash against Internet communication. It is not private. It probably never really will be completely secure. So if you are ok with the world (grandma, teacher, enemy) reading what you say, ok; if not, don't say it…not online at least! You can't run and you can't hide from anything bad you say online!

Politeness

A young boy got bit by a shark. Television crews came to film him in the hospital. He was so polite in his answers that someone asked him why. He said, "Even if you get bit by a shark…you have to be polite!"

---

what parents, teachers, neighbors, and others can do to help kids be good in a rotten apple world:

Express optimism. Point out the good, not the bad.

Model good behavior yourself. Remember: KIDS ARE WATCHING and LEARNING how to be a good (hopefully) adult from you.

Role play with kids. This is painless, even fun. It helps kids see how easy it is to be stupid or smart.

Praise good behavior, especially small things.

Critique gently. Remind kids there are better ways to do some things.

Talk things over. Really listen. Give kids the perspective of experience and maturity.

Respect kids. Their life is hard, too.

Help young people focus on good things to do–volunteering, helping others, being a good neighbor just for the heck of it.

Discuss current events. Respect kids' opinions. Ask what they think and why.

Enjoy kids' company. Appreciate the joy of their youth.

AND MOST OF ALL, BE WILLING TO TALK ABOUT ANYTHING AND EVERY-THING. IF YOU CAN'T DO THAT, FIND SOMEONE WHO WILL DISCUSS TOUGH STUFF WITH YOUR KID!

Sherry's Advice!

Good moms have the best ideas because they love their kids so much. Good moms who have been through a lot with their kids have the best, best advice. Here are Mom Sherry's ideas she felt would be helpful to all kids, and for parents to share with their children.

Bad Company Corrupts Character: Pick your friends and acquaintances well. "Guilt by association" is not just some idle phrase. A young man was driving a car, taking his friends to a store. Once inside the store, his friends robbed it. The young man went to prison for 25 years for driving the "getaway" car. He had no idea what his friends had even done. But he was still an accessory to the crime and deemed guilty under the law. That's another reason for the phrase, "Ignorance is no excuse of the law."

See Something/Say Something: Today, it takes a village (and that includes adults and kids) to be brave and speak up when they witness bullying, or any other bad thing. Never falsely accuse someone. But when you see something you know is not right, tell the right person. This is not tattling and it's best not to accost the person doing or saying bad things. Telling the right person would be helping the situation, not ratcheting it up, and preventing more of the same in the future. Safe for all. The right thing to do.

Truth or Consequences: For every action, there is a consequence, sometimes good, sometimes bad. Life is about choices. When you make bad choices you get bad consequences. But you can learn from your mistakes and avoid those bad choices next time.

Be OK with Who You Are!: If you could pick one mature attitude to have it would be this one. Don't seek the approval of everyone else—seek to act so that you approve yourself, that you have your own self-esteem, self-worth, and self-love. YOU ARE WORTH IT!

Miss Glenda's Internet Advice

The Internet and social media are not necessarily your friends. Yes, they can be fun, but they can also be full of false information. Don't believe everything you read or see!

Life is best lived in the real world, not the virtual world. There is a trend by a lot of kids to cut back (on their own) and get back outdoors, see friends, do things, and such—not just stare at the computer. Even psychologists and scientists believe that too much online can negatively affect your thought processes. Put family and friends first, school studies as an important priority, exercise and fun as essential, and staring at the screen (big or small) as the least thing you do each day.

Posturing: That's a big word that means you can "pose" as a cool kid on the Internet, or you can be a real kid in real life. What good does it do for people to "think" you are cool or tough or glamorous or whatever you try to portray yourself as online, when in real life you are just a normal, great kid? It's always best to be yourself, love yourself, and improve yourself. You can't fool all the people all the time. You really don't want to fool anyone. You just want to be the cool, great you in real life.

Not every kid is lucky enough to have parents who look over their shoulder, keep an eye on them, advise them, even fuss at them. If this is you, learn to practice good judgement, have perspective, and have discipline. What if your friends don't? Maybe you need new friends?

Learn to hold yourself accountable to yourself. After all, you are growing up, maybe faster than your peers. That could make them jealous or insecure. Let that be their problem. You be the best you can be. One day you will apply for a job, and no one will ask you, "Well, how much time did you waste on the Internet?"

Don't accept the negative influence of the Internet; BE the positive influence and example in real life—where it really counts.

PART FOUR: Good Kid Workbook Checklists

The end of the book for me, the author. The beginning of a better life for you, a good kid!

My First Checklist

I think the world is ☐ good/ ☐ bad/ ☐ good and bad.

I think that I am ☐ good/ ☐ bad/ ☐ good and bad.

I tend to hang out with ☐ good kids/ ☐ kids who may not be so good all the time.

I think trying to be my best:

☐ a. helps me

☐ b. helps everyone

☐ c. helps the world

☐ d. all of the above

On a scale of 1 to 10, I feel that I am usually this good. (Circle one.): 1 2 3 4 5 6 7 8 9 10

On a scale of 1 to 10, I think that the bad stuff I do is generally about here. (Circle one.): 1 2 3 4 5 6 7 8 9 10

My Goodness Self-Checklist

In general, I am:

☐ nice

☐ polite

☐ kind

☐ cooperative

☐ sharing

☐ caring

☐ generous

☐ patient

☐ complimentary

Usually I do not:

☐ bully

☐ criticize

☐ tease

☐ say hateful things

☐ be rude

☐ push or shove

☐ fight

☐ ignore people

☐ lie

My Friendliness Checklist

My friends ☐ do/ ☐ do not pressure me into doing things I should not do.

My friends ☐ are/ ☐ are not always getting into trouble.

My friends ☐ would/ ☐ would not hurt me.

I feel like these are friends I ☐ should keep/ ☐ should swap out for better friends.

I'd like to think I might have most of my friends ☐ for as short a time as possible/ ☐ forever.

I think my friends feel they ☐ can/ ☐ cannot trust me.

I know that I ☐ can/ ☐ cannot trust my friends.

My Good Choices/Bad Choices Checklist

I think that I should not choose things that:

- ☐ send me to jail
- ☐ send me to the principal's office
- ☐ get me expelled
- ☐ make my mom cry
- ☐ give me a bad reputation
- ☐ turn my friends against me
- ☐ hurt my future
- ☐ are unhealthy
- ☐ could send me to the Emergency Room
- ☐ would make me ashamed of myself
- ☐ would hurt someone else
- ☐ embarrass me
- ☐ I could not take back
- ☐ are a permanent solution to a temporary problem

My Good Habit Checklist

- ☐ I try not to tease people to hurt their feelings.
- ☐ I try not to say bad words.
- ☐ I try not to hang around with kids who do things that I know are bad.
- ☐ I try not to be a smart-aleck.
- ☐ I try not to lie, cheat, or steal.
- ☐ I try not to be rude.
- ☐ I try not to be someone I'm not.
- ☐ I try not to copy someone else just to be cool or part of the gang.

My Bad to-the-Bone Checklist

I know I am not perfect, but I prefer not to:

- [ ] lie
- [ ] cheat
- [ ] steal
- [ ] bully
- [ ] fight
- [ ] curse
- [ ] be mean
- [ ] be rude
- [ ] be sneaky
- [ ] get others into trouble

How Good Am I? Checklist

If there was a new kid in my class, I would:

- ☐ ignore them.
- ☐ figure someone else would be nice to them.
- ☐ be nice and ask them to sit with me at lunch.

I always assume that a new kid I meet:

- ☐ is a lot like me.
- ☐ would make a good friend.
- ☐ is stuck up and should be avoided.
- ☐ is new and so will just have to find their own friends.

When I meet someone new:

- ☐ I try not to draw conclusions just by their race, dress, name, or some other reason.
- ☐ I try to speak to them, learn their name, and include them at lunch or recess.
- ☐ I avoid them unless I see my friends being nice to them.
- ☐ I ignore them; I was new once and everyone ignored me.

Conflict Resolution Checklist

What is conflict?

A difference of opinion is a conflict. ☐ True/ ☐ False

A disagreement is a conflict. ☐ True/ ☐ False

A debate over something is a conflict. ☐ True/ ☐ False

I can avoid conflict by:

☐ walking away.

☐ listening and sharing my opinion, but not arguing.

☐ staying calm, even if the other person does not.

☐ being reasonable.

☐ agreeing when I can; disagreeing in an agreeable manner.

☐ not yelling or screaming.

☐ not belittling the other person's point of view.

☐ changing the subject.

☐ agreeing to disagree.

☐ not getting angry.

☐ understanding that there are two sides to everything.

☐ realizing I might be wrong.

My Relationship Drama Checklist

Here are some ways I could either get caught up in drama problems, or avoid them. Put a D for drama or an A for avoid.

- ☐ If someone makes a mountain out of a molehill, I could just have a tantrum and taunt them back.
- ☐ If someone tells a lie about me, I can just make up an even bigger lie about them.
- ☐ If I overhear someone bullying a person, I can join in and gang up on them.
- ☐ I can exaggerate so that no one can tell what is the truth.
- ☐ No matter what someone says, I can say the opposite, whether I believe it or not…just to make them mad.
- ☐ I can ignore someone when they are pretty much telling lies, even if other people believe them.
- ☐ I can laugh some things off.
- ☐ I can walk away and not listen.
- ☐ I can remember that this person is a drama king or queen and just steer clear of them.

My Trouble Checklist

I prefer to ☐ get into/ ☐ stay out of trouble.

I have found that ☐ good friends/ ☐ bad friends help me stay out of trouble.

I hang out with troublemakers because they are exciting. ☐ Yes/ ☐ No

I avoid troublemakers because even if I did not start something, I will have a hard time proving that. ☐ Yes/ ☐ No

If I see trouble, I run ☐ toward/ ☐ away from it.

My Anger Management Checklist

These three things really make me angry:

1. ______________________________

2. ______________________________

3. ______________________________

I try not to get too angry by:

☐ walking away.

☐ counting to ten.

☐ taking some time to think about things.

☐ forgetting the whole thing.

When I get angry, I want to:

☐ get even!

☐ get even, but know that is not the best idea.

When I am angry, I often:

☐ overreact.

☐ try not to overreact.

☐ I try not to jump to conclusions; maybe that person did not really mean what they said.

☐ I always jump to conclusions; I prefer to pick a fight.

I can usually distract myself from being angry by:

☐ getting away from the situation.

☐ thinking about something else.

☐ reading a book.

☐ finding a friend to complain to.

☐ kicking a soccer ball, hitting a baseball, or doing some other sport.

My Ego Checklist

- ☐ I have a BIG ego.
- ☐ I can keep my ego in check.
- ☐ I don't find it that hard to back down, walk away, turn the other cheek, or laugh something off.
- ☐ I always come out slugging; no one's gonna make a fool of me!
- ☐ I like to trade insult for insult.
- ☐ I don't feel like I have to be right all the time.
- ☐ If I know I am right, I figure that's all that matters; no sense trying to convince someone else, I figure.

Fruits of the Spirit Checklist

I am a kid, but I think I can have:

- ☐ love
- ☐ joy
- ☐ peace
- ☐ patience
- ☐ kindness
- ☐ goodness
- ☐ gentleness
- ☐ faithfulness
- ☐ self-control

My Blessings Checklist

I realize that every kid does not have the same thing. Here are some blessings that I am grateful for.

- ☐ a mom
- ☐ a dad
- ☐ a brother or brothers
- ☐ a sister or sisters
- ☐ a place to live
- ☐ food to eat
- ☐ a school to attend
- ☐ a good teacher
- ☐ friends
- ☐ health
- ☐ a neighborhood
- ☐ a peaceful country to live in
- ☐ safety
- ☐ a pet
- ☐ a grandmother
- ☐ a grandfather
- ☐ aunts and uncles
- ☐ cousins

- ☐ a bike
- ☐ toys
- ☐ a computer or access to one
- ☐ a cell phone
- ☐ a sport to play
- ☐ a hobby
- ☐ a best friend
- ☐ a church or other religious place to go to
- ☐ good neighbors
- ☐ clothes
- ☐ people who need me
- ☐ I can read
- ☐ I can write
- ☐ I am learning math

Other blessings:

____

____

____

My Likeability Checklist

I think most people like me because:

- ☐ I am friendly
- ☐ I listen to them
- ☐ I smile
- ☐ I offer to help them if I can
- ☐ I care about them and let them know I do
- ☐ I share with them
- ☐ I laugh with them
- ☐ I try to be nice
- ☐ I am not mean
- ☐ I do not bully
- ☐ I don't tell lies about them
- ☐ I don't tease them
- ☐ I don't pick fights

My Comparison Checklist

Here are the top three troubles I have:

1. ______________________________

2. ______________________________

3. ______________________________

Here are the top three troubles I would really hate to have:

1. ______________________________

2. ______________________________

3. ______________________________

My Good Ideas Checklist

Check which things to do that you believe would be a smart idea.

- ☐ Be nice to any new kid; they might need a friend.
- ☐ If you realize anyone around you is smoking, drinking, doing drugs, or anything else bad or illegal, leave!
- ☐ When I can, I will just turn the other cheek.
- ☐ Never be afraid to ask a trusted adult for help; that's what they are there for!
- ☐ Remember that I am trying to grow up, to mature, to be smarter.
- ☐ To use The Golden Rule as a good reminder of how to be good.
- ☐ To observe adults and copy good habits and avoid the bad habits you see them use.
- ☐ Avoid drama.
- ☐ Try to be happy.
- ☐ Don't whine or complain.
- ☐ Take some alone time. A little peace and quiet never hurt anyone.
- ☐ If I am ever bored, find something good to do.

- ☐ Not be embarrassed to be kind.
- ☐ Don't let people get under your skin.
- ☐ Be grateful and say so. "Thank you" is a big deal and easy to say.
- ☐ Realize that people are paying attention. You create your good reputation through your actions.
- ☐ Remember you have control over your actions.
- ☐ Love yourself. Love your age.
- ☐ Don't discriminate against anyone. They are different; you are different. Maybe that makes you the same?
- ☐ Remember things could always be worse.
- ☐ Remember there's always someone worse off than you are.
- ☐ Remember that God may have a better plan (and schedule) that you do!

My Parent Checklist

My parents may not know everything, but they know a lot. I can be a good kid when I:

- ☐ help my parents
- ☐ be patient with them; they can have a bad day, too
- ☐ listen
- ☐ obey
- ☐ be mature
- ☐ do good at school
- ☐ not argue over everything
- ☐ not criticize
- ☐ help my brothers and sisters
- ☐ not get in trouble
- ☐ try to love them as much as I hope they love me
- ☐ thank them

My Wisdom Checklist

I think I will be mature when:

- ☐ I listen to adults and take good advice.
- ☐ I do not try to be a know-it-all.
- ☐ I can keep my mouth shut when needed.
- ☐ I am trustworthy.
- ☐ I am humble.
- ☐ I do not do foolish things.
- ☐ I learn from my mistakes.
- ☐ I am a good friend.
- ☐ I am polite.
- ☐ I give up childish ways that I have outgrown.
- ☐ I am busy and do useful things.
- ☐ I have a plan for my future.
- ☐ I don't act selfish.
- ☐ I am a good role model.
- ☐ I think more about giving than getting.
- ☐ I show appreciation.
- ☐ I learn to control my temper.

My "I think I'll try these!" Checklist

- ☐ Teach myself to have more self-discipline.
- ☐ Have a positive attitude.
- ☐ Don't be so cynical.
- ☐ Try journaling to get my feelings out.
- ☐ Read some self-help books.
- ☐ Be more self-motivational.
- ☐ Give myself a break more often.
- ☐ Set mini-goals to get to my bigger goals.
- ☐ Set bigger goals.
- ☐ Be more flexible.
- ☐ Have confidence.
- ☐ Don't be smug, cocky, arrogant.
- ☐ Practice controlling my impulses.
- ☐ Practice being cool, calm, and collected.
- ☐ Don't be a cyberbully or put up with it.
- ☐ Spend less time on my digital devices and more time living my life.
- ☐ Don't be so self-absorbed.

What are your ideas?:

Good Kid Glossary

attitude: A good one is the only kind to have!

bully: What definitely NOT to be!

care: About yourself, your family, your friends, even your enemies!

determination: What you set your mind to you can achieve!

empathy: Put yourself in the other person's shoes; if they pinch you'll better understand how they might feel!

forgive: Everyone can't be right or perfect or good all the time; forgive and allow others to forgive you!

good: You don't have to be an "angel" to be good. Just be good as you can, when you can, all you can, to everyone you can!

happy: A good person is generally a lot happier than a bad, nasty, ornery person!

imagine: Imagine how the other person feels; you might have more in common than you think!

justice: Life may not be fair, but it's only fair for you to be fair!

kick: Do not kick someone when they are already down; that's mean. If they are down, reach out a hand and pull them up!

laugh: Sometimes life is just funny. Stupid, maybe. Dumb, perhaps. But funny. It's good to laugh!

mercy: That's giving someone a break when they've done you wrong. Maybe they are sorry and just won't say so. Maybe they wish they could take back what they said or did, but don't. Give them the benefit of the doubt, when you can, and hope others will do the same for you!

nevermind: Sometimes when you want to do or say or think something bad, just think "Oh, nevermind!" instead. It probably isn't worth it to be rude or ugly, anyway. (Sometimes, when a car pulls out in front of me, I want to say bad words. Instead I say, 'Oh, nevermind!'" and even laugh. Maybe that person is lost, an idiot, or blind? But it's less stress to just go on and forget about it. Really!)

opportunity: It might sound crazy, but often a bad thing is an opportunity to make a friend. If you make a mistake and apologize, sometimes the other person says, "No problem!" Or, "No problem, wanna go get some pizza?"

pardon: If you went to jail and were sorry for what you had done, you might just wish someone would give you a pardon. So why don't you be nice and pardon people for much smaller infractions than, say, robbing a bank or murder? Would it really be all that hard? (See the power a good person has!)

quick: A good person is quick to do the right thing and not bother thinking of reasons not to or what the other person has done to them in the past.

remember: Remember that when you pick a fight or start bad stuff, it's likely that you'll be the one who gets hurt. So, ouch!, don't do that to yourself!

satisfaction: Comes from being good. It just does!

temper: Watch your temper; don't let it get you in trouble!

understand: You can pretend you know how to be good, or act like you don't have a clue. But understand that the only person you'll be fooling is yourself!

vision: Have a vision for how good you want to be and work toward that. It's a process. One bad does not make a lifetime of bad; one good is not good enough.

wow!: If you have read this far, then wow!: I am impressed. You are good!

X: We all know "X marks the spot" so put an X on your heart and remember that is the spot that counts the most!

you: You will be surprised what being good brings you. But a better way to say it is that you don't want to be surprised what being bad brings you!

zip it: Don't let your mouth get you into trouble! But master your mouth, and half the BE GOOD battle is won.

Is is Really a Rotten Apple World?

The "world" is evil--it is rotten. That's the cold, hard truth. But there's another truth: we are to make it a better place everywhere we go/are. We are carriers of light in a world of darkness. This book is one way of shedding some light on some real stuff.

—Sherry Moss

There are bad apples...but you don't have to be one!

One bad apple don't spoil the whole bunch.

—Mos Def, hip-hop artist

A few bad apples are no reason not to visit the orchard.

—Lauren Weisberger, novelist

All badness is spoiled goodness. A bad apple is a good apple that became rotten.

—Fulton J. Sheen, theologian

The rotten apple spoils his companion.

—Benjamin Franklin

A Special Note From the Author

This book was written with an acute awareness that so many children have serious problems and issues at quite young ages. Also, that there are many more serious problems and issues that seem beyond the scope of this book. Polls and studies show that children of a wide age range know about most of these issues. Of course, recent news headlines show us that there are always new problems coming online that we must also cope with. A recent KIDS issue of *Time Magazine* covered the Parkland, Florida school shooting and resulting activism by students there and across the nation. It noted that events are being watched closely by elementary and middle school as well as high school students. I just want my readers to know that whether it's suicide, gender identity, "cutting" (intentionally harming oneself), rape, pregnancy, and even the new "incel" situation, NOTHING should be off the table to discuss. If a child is old enough to ask a question, they deserve an answer. I felt that some subjects would need to be delved into much deeper than this book allows to truly help readers. I encourage parents to be brave and open to discussions on any subject. And I encourage kids of any age to ask for help for any situation. Ask and ask again. It's your job to be a kid; it's our job to help you.

Keep asking until you do find help. You do not need to suffer, feel shame, or feel alone. If you have a problem, you can be SURE that others do, too, and that there is always a community of help. That's what makes this NOT a rotten apple world.

BE MORE OF YOU AND LESS OF THEM.

—via Ella on Instagram

YOU CAN
DO THIS!

About the Author and Illustrator

Carole Marsh Longmeyer has been writing for children and adults for forty years. The author has won many awards for her work and was named Georgia Author of the Year for Middle School Readers. She raised two children on her own and has six grandchildren, boys and girls ages 5 to 22. "As a kid in Atlanta, we moved a lot and I attended many schools, often moving during the school year. I started working in tenth grade. I have experienced or encountered many of the issues that I write about and admire kids of all ages who struggle, overcome, and go on to help others do the same." She lives with her rescue dog, Coconut, in Beaufort, SC.

Susan Van Denhende has a BFA from The Savannah College of Art and Design. She has been designing books for over three years and has been reading and drawing for as long as she can remember. She loves that she can use her gifts and interests to benefit kids. "As a kid, I read anywhere and everywhere I could--in the car, on the playground, in the cafeteria at lunch, even in the halls as I walked around school. The books I read had such a profound impact on my life, and I love that, through books, my work can impact the lives of kids I've never even met." Susan currently lives with a large collection of books in Jacksonville, FL. You can view more of her work at auroradoesart.com.